Tips From A Talent Agent

Practical Advice for Actors

By
Dr. Rebecca Fichter Hale

Tips From A Talent Agent

Practical Advice for Actors

By Dr. Rebecca Fichter Hale

Rock Press

Tips From A Talent Agent
Practical Advice for Actors
Dr. Rebecca Fichter Hale
Book Copyright © 2021 Dr. Rebecca Fichter Hale
Library of Congress Control Number 2020952151

ISBN 978-0-9792736-2-9
Printed in the United States of America
First Edition

Published by Rock Press, A Division of American Bushido, Inc.
10760 London Street
Hollywood, Florida 33026 USA
www.Rock-Press.com

Direct inquiries and/or orders to the above address.

ACKNOWLEDGEMENTS

This book is dedicated to Lauren Swinney (February 25, 1923 – July 1, 2020), the oldest actress that this agent/writer represented. Lauren was such a treasure, a wonderful actress that the author had the privilege of representing for many years. Lauren truly was a genuine, kind person who was loved by many. She will be missed.

The author wishes to express sincere appreciation and many thanks to her talented publisher and close friend Tracey Broussard for believing in her and using her expertise to guide the author in completing this book. Tracey is a constant inspiration for the author.

The writer wishes to thank the following people for sharing their stories and comments: Leon Contavesprie, Hilda Garrison, Veleka Gray, Michael Shane Hughes, Sue-Dee Lazzerini, Shane LeCocq, Robyn Nolting, and Rene J.F. Piazza. Thanks also to Kristen and Shane Brooks for allowing the author to be the agent for their children.

Table of Contents

Overview of Book

Why did I become an agent? I taught school for forty-three years – Theatre, English, and Speech – to middle school, high school, and college students. At many of the schools where I taught, I was blessed to work with extremely talented students. Some of my former students majored in drama in college or attended professional drama schools and have gone on to professional acting careers. At one particular high school where I taught, local talent agents had heard how good my actors were, so they began attending my theatre productions. After performances, these agents would ask me to speak to the parents of such and such a student about having the agent representing that student professionally. After doing this for a few months, I thought to myself, "Why don't I become an agent?" That's exactly what I did in 1994, as I continued to teach school.

I love being an agent. I wrote this book to answer many of the questions that actors have posed to me. I also have examples of real situations that have happened to me and/or my actors at auditions and on the set. Preparation, Headshots and Resumes, Why An Actor Needs An Agent, Auditioning Tips, Do's and Don'ts of Acting, Tips for Parents, How To Book An Acting Job and a List of Important Terms That An Actor Should Know are included in this book.

While I am aware that putting words in all capitals can be interpreted as yelling, that is not my intention in this book. I have placed certain sentences in all caps because I would like the reader to pay particular attention to them. These are usually mistakes and pitfalls that I have seen actors make time and time again. I simply do not wish for you to make the same mistakes.

It is my hope that both the novice actor and the experienced actor will benefit from reading this book.

CHAPTER I

Preparation: Before the Audition

In order to begin a successful acting career, preparation is necessary. How does an actor prepare? Rarely does an actor get discovered by sitting in a mall. It's not impossible, but it's very unlikely. Yes, this has happened to, maybe, one person out of thousands of "would be" actors, but it is rare. For the other thousands who are pursuing acting careers, preparation is essential.

I get calls from actors all the time. When I ask if they have film and/or theatre experience, they brag that they have been an "extra" in one or more movies. Too many actors think that since they worked in a film as an "extra," they are now prepared for an acting career. This attitude is insulting to those actors who have studied their craft. I, however, do encourage new actors to work at least one day on a set as an extra. Some agents don't agree with me, but it's good to observe everything that happens on a set. Most major cities where movies are made have casting services for extra work. An actor can register with one of these casting services; no agent is needed.

As an agent, I'm looking for actors (for adults) with film credits, television credits, commercial credits, and/or many theatre credits. How does an actor get to the point of having these necessary film and/or theatre credits? What preparation is necessary?

For young people, if you are in elementary or high school and your school offers a speech class and/or drama classes, take them. Join your school's drama club, if there is one. Audition for school plays, church plays, community theatre plays.

Remember to study for your other, non-drama classes, too. It is important to work hard in your other classes. Often if a child does not perform well in regular classes, the parent won't allow him or her to perform in plays after school. As a former teacher, I have had parents pull their children from a play because of poor grades. Acting in a play is hard work and requires discipline and commitment. Rehearsals often involve long hours after school and on weekends. Students with poor grades in any school subjects can't afford to spend long hours rehearsing for a play (or performing in a film and/or commercial). Therefore, it is crucial to study for all subjects and maintain good grades. What you learn in science, history, math, etc., enables you to be a more well-rounded person. This will help considerably in your acting. Good actors are intelligent human beings. An actor needs to be intelligent to interpret scripts.

Observe people in every-day life, such as at the grocery store and at the mall. Listen to the way different people speak and watch how they walk and carry themselves. This will help with characterization. Caution: don't stare at people (they may view you as threatening). Just observe discreetly.

For graduating high school students, you may want to major or minor in drama in college. Check out all the wonderful drama programs in the United States or abroad. If you live in the New Orleans area, we are blessed with excellent college theatre programs at Tulane University, the University of New Orleans, Loyola University, Dillard University, and in Baton Rouge, Louisiana State University. Since New Orleans is referred to as the "Hollywood of the South" in terms of movies and television shows being filmed here, New Orleanians don't have to leave here to pursue acting and directing careers. For actors in other parts of the country, there are many top-quality acting schools (I'm partial to N.Y.U.). With the Internet, it's so easy to research colleges and conservatories with excellent acting programs. If a regular college program or conservatory program doesn't interest you, you can still take drama courses as electives while you study a different major.

For other actors, continue to study your craft. Some actors are of the opinion that they know everything about acting, so they don't need to take classes ever. This is a mistake. The best actors continue to study their craft. One actor I represent told me he doesn't believe in attending workshops or classes (as if he knows everything about acting). The first audition I sent him on, he told me that he froze. He apologized to the casting director and to me. Granted, this could happen to experienced actors, but workshops and acting classes can help an actor prepare for these situations. If you are able, participate in weekly acting classes, taught by reputable teachers. Check a teacher's background. Where did the acting teacher get his or her training? Does the teacher have a drama degree from a university or professional school with a reputable acting program?

What professional acting credits does the teacher have?

A parent once told me she and her husband had spent $2,000 at a local modeling/acting school. When I questioned her about what her daughter was being taught for that money, she replied that the daughter was learning acting from a really good acting teacher. Further investigation revealed that the acting teacher had never even taken an acting class. True story! The point is do your homework.

If you can't afford regular acting classes, take workshops. One day or weekend workshops are offered all over the world by reputable acting teachers. Again, do your homework. Be selective about the type of workshop that will best suit your acting needs. Most one or two-day workshops are offered at reasonable prices. However, simply because an actor or acting teacher is from New York or California and is coming to New Orleans or Houston or St. Louis, etc., to teach a workshop doesn't mean this individual is automatically a wonderful teacher. He or she could be, but again, do your homework. Check credentials.

Also, some casting directors offer workshops. There are advantages to taking a casting director's class or workshop, especially if the actor gets to perform a monologue or scene. The casting director could consider the actor for a role he or she is casting in an upcoming project. When you get an agent, let your agent know if you attended a workshop taught by a casting director; this may be beneficial for you in the future.

Some agents teach workshops. I teach an "Acting for the Camera" Workshop three or four times per year. This is an excellent opportunity for new actors to be seen by an agent.

Some of you may live in areas with colleges that have really good film schools (New York University, University of Southern California, University of California – Berkeley, University of New Orleans, etc.). Since I have two degrees from there, I'll mention that the University of New Orleans Film School is ranked Number 4 in the country, as of this writing. Send the department head your headshot and resume (I will talk about headshots and resumes in another chapter) with a cover letter, stating your interest in auditioning for films directed by graduate film students. You probably won't get paid, but you will gain invaluable experience and a credit for a resume. Plus, some of these films will go to prestigious film festivals, such as Cannes or Sundance, where they are viewed by thousands of people. You never know what director may see you and like your work. This could lead to other acting opportunities for you. Also, acting in film shorts for the film festival circuit presents other opportunities for actors. One of my female actors performed in a short film that was shown in a film festival. That performance led to her being cast as the lead in a movie that was filmed in France.

Attend movies and plays. That is an excellent way to observe other actors. If your city is fortunate enough to have permanent or professional acting companies, such as Actor's Equity, the union for theatre actors, attend their plays. Don't neglect college productions, where one often can view wonderful acting. Young people should attend high school productions. If you live in New York City or you are able to visit there, attend Broadway plays. Attend lectures given by professional actors, acting teachers, casting directors, and agents, as well as seminars that professional actors may conduct on the internet.

Read plays, theatre publications, and acting books. Get recommendations from teachers as to which acting books suit your needs.

If you don't already have one, get a passport and keep it current. One of my actors lost out on a role in a production shooting in Europe because he didn't have a passport, and there wasn't enough time to get one. He would have been replacing an actor who was dropped from the cast at the last minute, so timing was crucial. Be prepared for situations like this.

In summary, to prepare for an acting career, an actor should do the following:

(1) Observe other actors by attending plays and movies;

(2) Read plays, theatre publications, and acting books;

(3) For high school and elementary students, join your school's drama club and audition for plays; also keep up your grades;

(4) If you are in college or a conservatory, major or minor in drama or theatre. If this isn't practical, major in another subject but take drama classes as electives;

(5) For all actors, audition for community theatre and church/religious plays;

(6) After you graduate from school, attend workshops, acting classes, and lectures;

(7) Inquire (by sending headshot and resume) about performing in college film productions and film festival productions;

(8) Observe people (discreetly) in general at malls, parks, the grocery store, etc., to view how they walk, talk, and carry themselves;

(9) Get a passport;

(10) Study your craft!

Headshots, Resumes, and Getting an Agent

HEADSHOTS

An actor will not get acting work without a good headshot and resume. What is a good headshot? There are different types of headshots. A basic headshot needs to look like the actor. When an agent submits a headshot to a casting director and the casting director requests for that actor to audition, the casting director wants the actor in the photo. One of my former students, age 14 at the time, had a glamorous photo of herself taken by a professional photographer at the local mall. It was a beautiful picture, but it made her look twenty-five years old. The student was upset with me when I said I couldn't submit that photo for acting work. Once again, the photo needs to look like the actor. Photos also need to be clear and in focus. The photo should focus on the actor and not extraneous elements.

If you are wearing glasses in your headshot, you should wear glasses at the audition. Be yourself. Think of adjectives and nouns that best describe the kind of characters you might easily portray. Ask your agent, acting teachers, and/or friends about the types of roles they could envision you playing. Then ask yourself if your headshot conveys this.

It is possible to submit photos with different looks or different expressions. A smiling expression for one headshot and a more serious expression for another headshot of the same actor give an agent options when submitting an actor. Females sometimes have headshots with different hairstyles, particularly if they have long hair, one shot with hair down and another shot with an updo hairstyle. Some males have headshots with and without facial hair. Other actors choose composite photos with three or four different looks on one page. These are all viable options.

Especially for the beginning actor, it is not necessary to spend a fortune on headshots. Most cities have photographers that charge a variety of fees to fit any budget. Actors must invest in their careers, so a decent 8x10 headshot is crucial. Do not use a selfie for your photo. A few years ago, only black and white headshots were considered acceptable. According to a few photographers that were questioned at that time, it was easier to touch up color photos, and black and white photos showed what the actor really looked like; therefore, black and white was the norm. However, times have changed. Today casting directors request color photos from actors. Give your agent two to five copies of your headshot. Be sure to keep copies for yourself. With advances in technology, it is not necessary to give an agent one hundred copies of your headshot. Recently, when I called an actor about an audition and reminded him to bring a headshot with him, he was in a panic since he had not kept any copies for himself. It is true that in order to get an audition, the agent would have submitted a headshot and resume to the casting director; however, some casting directors still request that actors bring a hard copy headshot and resume with them to the audition, so it's a good idea for actors to keep copies for themselves. One casting director told me he likes to put notes on the actor's headshot, so he asks for actors to bring a headshot to the audition. Also, for a callback, casting directors usually request multiple headshots; one copy is given to the casting director at the audition; other copies may be given to the director and the producer and/or the client for a commercial.

Since young children change appearance often as they grow older, their headshots should be updated often. If an actor of any age drastically changes his or her looks, such as changing hair color or cutting long hair very short, or gaining or losing a lot of weight, a new headshot is needed. If an adult actor still looks like his or her headshot from five years ago, it is acceptable to keep the same headshot. If not, update the headshot. One female actor I represent has natural blonde hair. The specifics of the role called for a natural blonde and emphasized this, among other attributes. She fit the description perfectly, so I submitted her headshot and resume. The casting director asked for her to audition. What I didn't know was that recently she had dyed her hair red, which is fine, except she didn't tell me this. An angry casting director called to complain and asked why I sent in an actor with red hair when she specifically requested a blonde. Keep your headshots current! Consult with your agent when you are deciding on new headshots.

I have signed actors who needed better or more professional headshots. They have agreed to do so; therefore, the headshots should be taken in a reasonable amount of time. Don't keep calling your agent with excuses (probably legitimate) as to why you haven't gotten the headshots taken. I realize that life happens, but if you want acting work, don't delay. Get those headshots.

RESUMES

An actor must have a clear, readable, one-page resume to put on the back of a headshot. Note that the resume must be one page only, unlike resumes for other types of work. Type your resume. Don't hand-write the resume, and don't scribble your resume on the back of your headshot. Standard information must be included, such as, the actor's name, agent's name, agent's phone number, height, hair color, and eye color. Listing your weight is optional. Once you get an agent, put your agent's name and phone number on the resume. Don't put your own phone number. For children thirteen and under, put date of birth. For actors fourteen and older, put an age range, such as 15-19. Don't put: "Age: 15." Maybe you are fifteen, but you could look fourteen. Casting directors aren't thinking you could play fourteen. It is also acceptable, especially for adults, not to put an age range at all. This is up to the actor. It is important to have your resume on file for auditions, so your agent doesn't need to email you your resume.

Be sure to list any acting or acting-related training you have had. For children, include elementary speech and acting classes, as well as any summer acting camps you have attended. For teenagers, include middle and high school speech and drama classes. If you have competed in speech tournaments, list that. For others, include college and conservatory classes. Always include workshops and list teachers/instructors of those workshops. Casting directors like to see that you have studied your craft. List any singing, dancing, martial arts, and stage combat training that you have. Specify your vocal range, the types of dancing that you are able to do (ballet, hip/hop, etc.), the types of martial arts that you do, and the type of stage combat training that you have, such as types of swords and rapiers that you can use well. If you are a stunt performer, list this.

Next, list your acting credits for film, theatre, commercials, educational videos, music videos, print work, and runway modeling. Experienced actors with a lot of credits should list major roles and most recent roles first. Actors with many commercial credits often will include this statement: List Furnished Upon Request. That is acceptable. The casting director can view your resume at the audition and ask you about other commercials.

Don't put dates on your resume. If the last credit you have is a film from two years ago and you list that year, a casting director may wonder why you haven't done any acting in two years. Include any special skills or interests you have, such as speaking a foreign language (fluently), playing a musical instrument (well), teleprompter experience (very valuable), or playing sports, particularly on a varsity team. Note: Only list sports if you can still actually play. A twenty-one year old who played high school varsity football a few years ago and is still in good athletic shape can list that he can play football. A forty year old who last played football at eighteen and is forty pounds overweight should not list that he can play football. The bottom line is if an actor can perform the skill convincingly (one doesn't have to be an athlete like Drew Brees or Tom Brady), list it on a resume. Regarding speaking a foreign language, one production had such attention to detail that an actor who could speak French fluently was requested. I have an actress who speaks French fluently, so she was hired. In the final cut, her dialogue was not audible; however, the director stated that he wanted a fluent French speaker in case anyone in the audience could read the lips of the speaker.

If an actor owns any costumes, particularly unusual costumes, list them. I once represented a woman who had been a queen in a Mardi Gras parade and still had the complete attire, including the crown and scepter. She was booked for a film because of that costume. Since so many television shows and films feature police officers, if an actor owns a police uniform, list it on a resume. I advise all male actors eighteen and over to purchase a plain black tuxedo (some stores have end-of-year sales), since I have had actors book roles because of owning a tuxedo. Owning a tuxedo also can be helpful for proms, balls, and society engagements you may attend. Women who own formal evening gowns should list this on a resume. Actors could find themselves in scenes where it is an advantage to own a tuxedo or evening gown. Male and female actors should invest in a good business suit. A business suit is appropriate wardrobe for many auditions that an actor will have.

If an actor has any special skills, definitely list these. I once represented a licensed airplane pilot; this should be listed on a resume. I also represented a female actor who was a sword-swallower; she was booked on more than one production because of this skill. Real nurses, doctors, and other medical personnel should list this as well, as should current and retired members of the military, police officers, and fire fighters. Actors with technical skills should list this. One never knows when these skills could contribute to an actor's being able to book a role.

I'm always asked whether or not an actor should list "extra" work on a resume. There is some disagreement among agents and casting directors about this. Personally, my advice is to list extra work on a resume until you get speaking roles or become a principal in a commercial. Also list stand-in work and "featured extra" work.

Word of advice: Do not pad a resume. Be honest. Don't invent credits if you think your resume isn't impressive. Many actors book work without having many credits, or any credits in the case of some beginning actors.

I have had actors book work the first time I sent them on an audition. What I don't like is for an actor to lie. I once had an actor who was seeking representation list a false credit for a little-known Henrik Ibsen play (*Brand*), so I questioned him about the play. I had performed in a production of this play. He obviously knew nothing about the play and had never acted in it. I chose not to be his agent. This may seem petty, but lies have a way of catching up with you. Be truthful! Don't lie!

Always check the spelling on your resume so every word is spelled correctly. Remember to keep all information current on the resume. If you appear in a commercial, film, etc., the new credit should be added to your resume once you have completed the project. In addition to updating your resume, if any vital information has changed (a change in hair color, for example), this should be listed on your resume. Once you are registered on Actors Access and Casting Networks, it will be easy to update your resume and headshot. Ask your agent about how to register and set up an account on both Actors Access and Casting Networks. Actors put their headshots and resumes on both these sites so that their agents can submit them for acting work.

Note: A resume gives you credit for the acting work you have done. If you happen to be cut out of a film or commercial when the final product is released, you are still able to list that as a credit on your resume because you completed the work for which you were hired.

Once you have been booked for acting work and have a few credits, you may want to invest in a demo reel (highly recommended). A demo reel is a professionally-produced collection of scenes that highlight an actor's best work in films (feature films, shorts, etc.), television shows, web series, or commercials. Reels can be an invaluable resource to aid your agent in promoting you. Note that this should be produced professionally and not recorded in your kitchen. It shows casting directors that an actor has experience in front of the camera. When actors are looking for an agent, they often will send their reels to prospective agents. The reel should be updated as an actor gains more credits. Actors also should put their reels on casting websites, such as Actors Access and Casting Networks. Reels definitely can help an actor book work. Actors who are interested in Voice-Over work should have a reel that features different types of voice-overs, such as commercials, announcements, audio books (books on tape). Check with your agent to view samples of these types of voice-over work. Voice-over reels also should be put on casting websites.

In summary, get a color headshot that looks like you and helps convey the types of roles for which you are most suited. Create a clear, readable, one-page, truthful resume. Once you book acting work, consider getting an acting reel. Have your agent view your acting reel when it is completed.

A sample headshot and resume are included in this book. You have a headshot and resume. Now you need to get an agent.

GETTING AN AGENT

I have heard some actors say that they didn't need an agent. They were of the opinion that an agent simply takes ten per cent of an actor's salary and does nothing for the actor. These actors are clueless and are making a big mistake. With all the websites offering to get acting work for actors, many actors are confused. An actor can get "extra" work on his or her own. However, to book a speaking role, an actor needs an agent. Agents risk their time, money, and reputations to promote actors to casting directors and, ultimately, to clients, directors, and producers.

Exactly what does an agent do? For actors who sign with an agent, an agent performs these tasks:

(1)   Reviews actors' resumes to make sure they are up-to-date and appropriate;

(2)   Reviews actors' headshots;

(3)   Reviews videos of actors' work – both for actors' reels and videos sent for auditions;

(4)   Submits actors to casting directors for roles;

(5)   Pushes actors to casting directors;

(6)   Makes countless phone calls and sends many emails to actors and casting directors;

(7)   Checks Breakdown Services and other audition sites for auditions;

(8)   Gives all available information to an actor when the actor has an audition;

(9)   Investigates the answers to numerous questions that actors have;

(10) Negotiates contracts when an actor has booked a role;

(11) Follows up with a production company, client, producer, or, possibly, the union when payment to an actor has been delayed;

(12) Encourages actors in their pursuit of an acting career.

An acting agent is like a real estate agent. If a realtor doesn't sell a property, the realtor doesn't make any money. If an actor doesn't book acting work, an agent doesn't make money. An agent could work for weeks getting auditions for actors, but again if the actor doesn't book the job, the agent doesn't make any money. Make no mistake about it. Agents work very hard. A professional actor knows he or she needs an agent to further his/her career. Reputable casting directors contact agents for professional auditions. Also, how an actor performs at an audition and on a set reflects on the agency. Agents are paid ten per cent for union (SAG-AFTRA) jobs. Actors need to focus on what they need to do for their ninety per cent of the pie by continuing to improve as actors and book the job.

How does an actor get an agent? Investigate, by using the Internet, which agents are in your area. Acting friends and acting teachers also can recommend agents. Check an agent's website, which often will give information about how an actor can submit to the agent, or telephone the agent to find out: (1) if the agent is accepting new actors; and (2) what the agent's submission procedure is. I accept submissions by email and regular mail, but not all agents accept unsolicited submissions. I discover acting talent in a number of ways: by attending theatre productions as often as possible; through teacher recommendations; by attending showcases; and from acting classes and workshops I have taught. I also interview some actors based on their headshots and resumes. If the actor is appearing in a play or showcase, he or she can send a postcard or an email to an agent, listing the pertinent information.

Some agents may ask an actor to prepare a scene before meeting with the actor. It is an excellent idea for an actor to have a dramatic scene, a comedic scene, a dramatic monologue, and a comedic monologue in his or her repertoire. If you are a theatre actor, have a Shakespearean monologue prepared. If you are a musical theatre performer, have 18 bars of a song prepared.

Once an agent has agreed to sign an actor, the actor usually will sign a contract. Do keep in touch with your agent by calling or emailing every couple of weeks, just to "check in." Talent agents work very hard for their actors, so actors should send the commission money the agent is owed in a timely manner. Trust in your agent's judgment! She does know what she is doing. There should be mutual respect between an agent and actor. An actor must trust that the agent is submitting him or her for any role for which the actor is suited.

A question that I have been asked from almost all actors I have signed is how often can they expect to be sent on an audition. That is an impossible question to answer. I am not a production company; therefore, I don't have any control as to what type of production is shooting or which types of roles are in the production. Not every actor can play every role written. I love Meryl Streep, but even she can't play every role ever written. What I truthfully can promise my actors is I will submit them for any role that they fit.

What should an agent expect from an actor?

(1)   Stay in touch with your agent. You are not bothering him or her. Ideally, email every two or three weeks. If it's important to talk to the agent on the phone, say that in the email, and the agent will call you. Have excellent communication with your agent;

(2)   Be thoroughly prepared for all auditions for which the agent is sending you;

(3)   Be professional;

(4)   If an actor is delayed for an audition (make every effort not to have this happen), call your agent as soon as possible;

(5)   Inform your agent if you change phone numbers and/or email address. Be sure to give your agent an accurate email address and accurate phone number. Your agent has to be able to reach you;

(6)   Have your headshot and resume updated;

(7)   When you are asked to submit an Eco Cast Audition (a website through Breakdown Services, where an actor is asked to submit a video audition directly to a casting director), check the deadline the audition must be submitted. The time and date of submission are very important.

(8)   If an actor changes his or her name. inform your agent as soon as possible. Be certain that the name on your resume and headshot matches the official name that is on your SAG-AFTRA account (if you are in the union). Also, if you become eligible for SAG-AFTRA and you join, let your agent know as soon as possible so she or he won't submit you for non-union work.

(9)   If you decide to part ways with your agent and get another agent, have the courtesy to tell your agent. Don't let the agent find this out from Actors Access (happened to me).

(10) If you intend to travel out of town for any length of time and won't be available to audition and/or accept acting work, let your agent know this so she or he won't waste time submitting you for work that you can't accept.

(11) If you move out of state, inform your agent as soon as possible. I once represented an actor from Oklahoma. I called him about an audition in Oklahoma. He had neglected to tell me that he currently was living in New York for two months and then moving permanently to California. You must communicate with your agent.

(12) If an actor has a drastic change in appearance, let your agent know this. Twice female actors were pregnant (one was expecting twins), and neither let me know until I called about auditions. Certainly, pregnant women can be cast in projects, but these two roles were not for pregnant women.

(13) If you are unavailable for auditions because of health reasons (you need to have surgery; you broke your leg, etc.), inform your agent.

(14) Check your email every day. One of my actors accused me of not submitting him for work. He left a phone message stating that he was sitting around waiting for an audition. The irony of this situation is I had indeed left an email and a phone message to him about an audition and not heard back from him. He had failed to check his email (he later found the email I had sent) and his phone messages. Agents can't do the impossible! Actors, be responsible!

(15) If you ask your agent to submit you for a role out of state, make certain if you are cast that you can accept the role, even if it means re-locating (such as, for a television series).

Just because an actor doesn't hear from his or her agent doesn't mean the agent isn't working very hard for the actor. Agents want actors to get as many auditions as possible and to book as many acting jobs as possible. I once taught an acting class where three of the men in the class had been called by me the day before to audition for a film. The two women in the class wanted to know why I hadn't called them to audition. There were no women's roles for which the two women were suited. Agents can't invent roles to keep everyone happy.

You have acting training. You have a headshot and resume. You have an agent. Now you are ready to book acting work.

CHAPTER III

Let's Book Acting Work: Auditioning Tips, Proper Auditioning Procedures, and Set Etiquette

The process for professional auditioning works as follows: For films and television, producers hire casting directors to submit the best talent. For commercials, the client usually hires the casting director. For some productions for films and television, often a local casting director is employed to submit local actors to be considered for roles; for other productions, both a national casting director who usually will cast "name" actors and a local casting director will be hired. Casting directors contact agents and send them the breakdown of all available roles being cast. Often the "name" actors for a film or television series have been cast already. The agent then submits, in most cases electronically, headshots and resumes of actors who fit the roles being cast. That is why headshots and resumes are crucial; without them, it is difficult for an agent to get an audition for an actor.

The casting director then calls or emails the agent, requesting certain actors to audition. The agent then calls, emails, or texts (sometimes all three) the actor. ACTORS, CHECK YOUR EMAIL EVERY DAY! Actors, remember to let your agent know AS SOON AS POSSIBLE if you have changed your phone number or email address.

The actor must get all possible information about the audition from the agent, such as the following:

(1)   Name of project;

(2)   Type of project (film, commercial, television series, etc.);

(3)   Location of audition;

(4)   Description of role;

(5)   Storyline;

(6)   Name of casting director;

(7)   Name of director, producer, or client (if available);

(8)   Wardrobe for audition;

(9)   Date of audition and time of audition;

(10) Date of filming;

(11) Location of filming (local or out of town);

(12) Any other information the agent can supply.

In some instances, the agent is given only minimal information; in other cases, the agent can supply the actor with many more details. For some films, the entire screenplay is available; if so, the actor should read the entire screenplay. This will be valuable in analyzing the role for the audition. Particularly for a television series, often only the "sides" are available. Sides are pages, usually one or two, of scenes from a film or television script, used for auditions.

Occasionally, an actor and, sometimes, the agent will be required to sign a confidentiality agreement before the audition (to keep the plot secretive). This is called a Non-Disclosure Agreement (NDA). DO NOT POST THE SIDES OR ANY INFORMATION ABOUT THE PRODUCTION ON SOCIAL MEDIA. DO NOT POST THE VIDEO AUDITION YOU ARE SENDING TO A CASTING DIRECTOR TO ANY SOCIAL MEDIA

SITE. If you do this, your actions could prevent you from booking an acting job.

In some instances, the casting director does not reside in the same state where the project will be filmed. Often these casting directors will request that for the first audition the actor submit a taped audition. Also, the taped audition is beneficial to the actor when, for whatever reason, the actor is not available to attend an in-person audition. Therefore, it's crucial for an actor to know how to submit a taped audition. Make certain that your taped audition is done indoors and not outdoors. There are too many distracting outside noises (cars, planes, animal noises, etc.), so your audition should be recorded inside. Also, it should be recorded horizontally and not vertically. It would be beneficial for the actor to purchase a solid backdrop to use when taping, rather than simply using a sheet. It is possible to purchase an inexpensive backdrop, so investigate this. A solid backdrop is important because the focus should be on the actor and not other elements in the room, such as pots and pans if the actor records in his or her kitchen.

An assistant casting director attended a recent acting workshop that I taught and provided excellent insight to the actors. She stressed how crucial it is when taping an audition that the actors follow the directions explicitly. The casting director for whom she works will reject an audition (no matter how good the audition is) if the actor has not followed the taping instructions exactly as given. She also made a point of telling the actors that they must adhere to the deadline given for submission. Submitting a taped audition even five minutes passed the time deadline could cause the casting director to disregard the actor's audition. Actors, allow yourselves enough time to submit the video auditions.

When your agent tells you the upcoming dates of the project for which you are auditioning, be certain to check the possible dates (dates of filming can change) very carefully. If you have any conflicts with filming dates, tell your agent. Your agent probably will tell you not to audition.

If there are only certain days that you are available to audition (because of your work schedule at another job), let your agent know this. Believe it or not, one of my actors can audition only on a Monday; however, if cast, he definitely will take off of work from his job. Do keep in mind (my actor knows this) that this is a difficult situation for an agent, and as an agent, I try to do my best, but it is often almost impossible for this to work. I know actors in California and New York probably find this situation incredulous because you consider yourselves full-time actors, but in other parts of the country, actors have to work so-called "regular jobs" to pay their bills. Therefore, this situation isn't that uncommon.

If an actor is asked to audition for a commercial where a food product is involved and the actor has an allergy to that product (such as, being allergic to peanuts or seafood), the actor should be totally honest with the agent about this, so the agent will not submit the actor for this audition. A breakdown may specify that an actor will need to eat meat in a commercial if booked; if an actor is a vegetarian, the agent needs to know this. Similarly, if an actor has an aversion to a product, business, etc., in a commercial, the actor should tell his or her agent. One of my actors had a major issue with an apartment rental company. I wanted to send him on an audition for a commercial for this company, but when I heard his story, I agreed that he shouldn't be submitted for this audition. Actors must communicate with their agents about possible conflicts regarding products or situations like the ones mentioned. It could be disastrous for an actor not to mention a food allergy, get booked for a food commercial, and then become ill on the set.

Do your homework. After your agent tells you the product name for a commercial audition, research the company. You would do this for a non-acting job interview. One of my actors had an audition for a tractor company. He knew nothing about tractors, but his father did, so he asked his father, who had owned two tractors, about tractor lingo – volume, density, etc. He felt confident that he could answer basic questions about tractors, which would help for his audition. The woman who auditioned with him was amazed that he knew so much about tractors; he was amazed that she knew nothing and didn't bother to do any research. The same actor, SAG-AFTRA actor Leon Contavesprie, auditioned for the role of a reporter in a film about a real person in Mississippi, a football player who was severely injured in a game years ago. Leon watched a documentary about the football player. The assistant casting director told the actor he was the only actor who did his homework.

If the audition for a commercial is for a store, such as Best Buy or Wal-Mart, go to the store and notice what the employees are wearing. Your agent may give you an example of wardrobe, but if you can, observe what employees wear.

Treat every audition as if it is a job interview. If you were interviewing for a job with Amazon, you would research the company. If you are able, get some background information on the people involved in the production, such as the casting director, director, writer, and producer. Find out what other films the director has directed. What else has the writer written? If the screenplay for a film is based on a novel, find the novel and read it. This is all part of being prepared for the audition.

If words or phrases in the sides are unfamiliar, investigate the meanings and pronunciations. Don't ever attend an audition not knowing the accurate pronunciation of a word or phrase. The same is true for "period pieces" (a film that is set in another time period other than the current one). Research the time period, paying particular attention to any colloquialisms that may have been used then and are not used now. If the subject matter of the film is a real person, research everything you can find about the person.

If the role calls for the actor to use an accent or dialect, research the appropriate accent or dialect. The Internet, using U-tube or other sites, can help with that. Casting directors will be impressed that you learned an accent or dialect for the audition, even though often on sets there will be a dialect coach to help the actor.

Don't try to make a small part more than it is. Most casting directors will tell the actor to keep it simple, that less is more on the small parts. On a television series, your responsibility as a guest actor is to feed the scene, to feed the series regular. The scene is almost always about the series regular, not the actor with one or two lines. Casting directors often send this note to agents: "Tell your actors NOT to chew the scenery." In other words, don't over-emote. For films and television, an actor doesn't have to be "big" as he or she would be on stage. Be natural and keep it simple.

Write down very carefully all information that your agent gives you. Don't waste your agent's time by calling to ask him or her to repeat information already given. Do call, however, if you are not clear about the information, or if you have a question about your role (interpretation, approximate age of character, if not stated, etc.). Know how to get to the audition; this is much easier now because many people have a GPS. However, if you are concerned that you could get lost, check out the location a day or two before the audition. It is always good to be prepared. I have had actors call me because they are on their way to the audition and lost the address; be responsible.

Regarding wardrobe for the audition, at times the agent receives a detailed description of how the actor should dress for the audition; at other times, very little, if any, wardrobe description is given. Actors often can get an idea of what to wear from the character description. In general, avoid wearing all-black or all-white to an audition. Since most auditions are taped, wearing all-black or all-white makes an actor look like he or she is blending in with the scenery. You don't want to blend in with the scenery; you want to stand out. However, I once had an audition for teen actors to portray "gang members," and the casting director specified for the actors to dress in all-black; there are exceptions to everything. In general, the best colors to wear to an audition are blue (aqua, teal, turquoise; not navy because it's too dark); green (any shade but neon green); yellow; pink; and beige. Of course, black or navy pants would work if you wear a shirt or blouse in another color, preferably bright. Don't wear a solid red dress (even though it could be a beautiful red dress), as on videotape, red can create a more pattern (squiggly lines). Don't wear distracting jewelry. You don't want the attention on your jewelry and not on you.

Wear appropriate clothes to an audition. Clothes should be clean and fit well. Don't wear clothes so tight that bulges show (unless for some reason that works for the role). Don't wear clothes with logos or school names; as silly as it may seem, a casting director could be prejudiced against a certain school, so don't give the casting director a reason not to cast you. Don't wear a shirt with a product name on it. You might have a shirt with "Pepsi" on it, and you might be auditioning for a Coke commercial. Coke and Pepsi own a lot of other companies. Again, don't give a casting director (or client) a reason not to cast you.

Hair should be clean, neat, and out of your eyes. The way to style your hair could vary according to the role for which you are auditioning. Of course, unconventional hairstyles will work if the role calls for that. An actor may be auditioning for a role where an unusual hairstyle, make-up look, etc., would be an advantage. Fingernails should be nicely trimmed, neat, with clear or conservative nail polish. Your hands may be photographed handling the advertiser's product. You may be asked to hold up your hands during an audition. There are exceptions. A role may call for the actor to have extremely long nails, or nails in bold colors or nails with patterns, etc. Tattoos and piercings are popular now, so a casting director may request an actor that has these. However, if you are auditioning for a more conservative role, cover the tattoos and remove the piercings.

All women's makeup should fall into the category known as "light street makeup," unless told otherwise. Lipstick should be conservative for some roles (doctor, lawyer, soccer mom) but bolder for others (exotic dancer, the sexy flirt, etc.). If in doubt, ask your agent. Men with beards and mustaches should keep them neat, unless the role calls for an actor with a scraggly beard. Men without facial hair should not have a beard line (my late father referred to this as "five o'clock shadow"). It may be necessary to shave again midday if you have an audition late in the day. Of course, a beard line may be appropriate for a certain role.

Dark lines and shadows around the eyes and slight blemishes can be erased with a cover-up makeup, but be sure that it blends well with your skin. Blemishes are what give our faces character, so you might not want to correct or change anything about your appearance, which is fine.

Good hygiene is important. Do wear deodorant and/or an antiperspirant. However, avoid wearing perfume, after-shave, or cologne at an audition. A casting director could be allergic to your cologne, after-shave, or perfume. A casting director recently sent all agents an email, stating that her office workers were highly allergic and asked agents to relay this information to their actors.

What should an actor bring to an audition? Bring your headshot and resume (multiple copies, if you are requested to do so). Bring a pen for filling out information. Know your height, weight, clothing sizes, and measurements. You may be asked to supply hat and glove sizes. If you don't know, go to a department store and try on a hat and a pair of gloves, so you will know these sizes. Know your agent's phone number. Wherever "phone number" is requested, list your agent's phone number. An item that you should purchase and bring with you is an appointment book (or if you can record information on your phone, that is acceptable). Keep an accurate record of every commercial audition, film audition, photo session, meeting with your agent. Also, buy a small notebook to log information about anything and everything that might someday help you in this business. Write down the names of casting people that you meet, as well as names of their assistants. Anything that can give you an edge over other actors may mean the difference between working and not working.

Regarding the use of props at an audition, I have questioned some casting directors about this, and they have said the actor should not bring props to an audition. At the very least, if your character is supposed to be talking on a phone, pantomime holding a phone to your ear. Don't even use your cell phone.

On your way to the audition, be happy with your wardrobe, hair, and makeup. It's too late to change them, so be satisfied with your selections. Allow enough time to get to the audition. There is always traffic, regardless of where you live. If, however, you are running late, CALL YOUR AGENT. The agent then can call the casting director and give an explanation as to why the actor is late. Sometimes the casting director will be sympathetic and other times angry, but at least the agent can inform the casting director that the actor is running late. You may feel a little nervous as you ride or walk to the audition, especially for your first few auditions; remember that this happens to everyone! The nervous feeling is adrenaline, which is a good thing. Use it as a positive. Take deep breaths to relax. Smile to yourself; it may become a habit. A vocal warm-up is one of the most vital things to do before an audition. Before approaching the audition location, pick out a speech, poem, song, or tongue-twister that you know the words to and recite it.

Once you arrive at the audition, sign in. There will be a sheet for this purpose. PRINT your name and the name of your agent: HALE TALENT (if I represent you). Know your agent's phone number, if this is asked. DO NOT LIST YOUR OWN PHONE NUMBER. You have an agent for a reason.

Sit quietly in the waiting room. This is not the time to socialize. There is nothing wrong with telling another actor, "Hello," but don't get into a big conversation with other actors in the waiting room. It can be very disruptive to the actors who are auditioning, possibly in the next room. Waiting rooms are usually small areas with not quite enough chairs for all the people who wish to occupy them. Just wait until a chair is vacant. Use the time to go over the "sides" (a piece of the script or copy) or to get composed. According to SAG-AFTRA actor Rene J.F. Piazza, "I'm hired to do a job. I'm not going to chat with everybody just to impress people." Some actors do like to brag about all the acting work they have done; some actually do this deliberately to "psyche out" the other actors, especially less experienced actors. Don't do this and don't allow this to upset you. Quite often producers are looking for a new face, someone who hasn't been seen a lot. Don't be awed by anyone. The face you recognize from a million commercials may have an over-exposure problem, and you may be better suited for this commercial. As an agent, I would not send you on an audition if I didn't think you had a chance of booking the job. I don't want my time wasted, nor do I want to waste the time of a casting director. You have as much chance of booking the job as anyone else, so don't get nervous when another actor has a much longer resume than you have, or starts talking about all the credits he or she has. One of my actors was at an audition when a well-known local actor walked into the waiting room, saw all the actors, and then proceeded to tell everyone in the room that they could all go home because he was booking the job. This is very rude and can have a damaging effect on other actors. Don't allow that to happen to you. Also, do NOT chew gum at an audition!

Turn off cellphones or put them on silent once you are in the waiting room One of my actors was at an audition when another actor in the waiting room proceeded to have a long, very loud conversation with his girlfriend, asking her if she wanted to say, "Hello," to the other actors. VERY UNPROFESSIONAL!

If any actors smoke, a word of advice: Don't smoke right before going on an audition (even if smoking calms your nerves). There are some casting directors who have a strong aversion to cigarette smoke and don't like for an actor to smell like smoke at an audition. One of my actors was chastised and embarrassed by a casting director for smelling like smoke at an audition. He had smoked in his vehicle on the way to the audition.

When your name is called to audition, be polite. Greet the casting director with a smile. Have good eye contact. Because of Coronavirus, Influenza Season, and other health issues, the days of shaking hands with the casting director, director, producer, etc., probably have ended. However, an actor can nod to acknowledge these people and, certainly, still can have good eye contact. Listen to directions and try to relax. Do not start the audition with an apology. The casting director does not want to hear that an actor just got the sides because his or her computer was broken, or he was late for the audition because his ride didn't show up. At an audition where I later booked an industrial film, a beautiful woman walked in (I didn't think I had a chance of booking the job when I saw her), and she proceeded to tell everyone in the room that she was late because she had to breast-feed her new baby. That's great that she had a new baby, but we didn't need to hear that. By making excuses, the actor is setting up the expectation that the audition is going to be bad.

The casting director probably will ask you to stand on your mark (usually an X marked with tape) and then slate. For SLATING, listen how the casting director and/or videographer wants you to slate. The actor always says his or her name. Then the slating can vary. Some casting directors want an actor to state agent's name and actor's height. Some just ask for height. Often for child actors, casting directors will ask the child to give his or her age. For adult actors, you shouldn't be asked your age. Remember to speak clearly, loudly, slowly, and distinctly. Particularly for commercials, the client may view hundreds of actors that have been videotaped. If the actor doesn't speak clearly, the client will move to the next actor on the tape. Look directly into the camera when slating, pretending the camera is your best friend. Some questions you are asked may sound foolish. However, on some occasions the casting director is trying to relax you, and maybe what the casting director is asking you to do actually takes place in the commercial or film. It is also possible that the casting director wants to see if the actor can take direction. Say the lines in the copy exactly as written. Clients pay advertisers a lot of money to write copy for commercials, so don't improvise the copy unless told to do so. The same is true for the sides in a film or television series. Say the lines as written. I can't stress enough how important it is to listen to any direction the casting director gives you. You may be asked to say the lines a second or third time in a different way. Some actors think they must have done something wrong if this happens. This is actually good because the casting director liked something about your performance, or else he or she wouldn't have you audition in a different way. Either that, or you "nailed" the audition the first time and were perfect, so the casting director doesn't need you to perform the lines again. This could happen, too. Remember that if you don't understand something that you are asked to do, by all means, ask the director for clarification. Don't wait for the audition to end and then realize you didn't understand something you were asked to do.

When the casting director says, "Thank you," or lets you know the audition is finished, leave, thanking him or her. Don't linger! DON'T ASK QUESTIONS! ("When will I find out if I booked the role?" "How much does this job pay?") DON'T ASK QUESTIONS! Leave with confidence and a smile! Let your agent answer any questions you may have after the audition. If other actors are entering the audition room as you leave, don't stop to chat! If someone coming into the room asks how the audition went, don't answer. Keep moving out of the room. If you think you didn't audition well and you tell this to an actor entering the room, the casting director (and others in the room, possibly the director and producer) can hear you say this and are left wondering why you didn't audition well for them, so don't say anything. Remember the casting director wants you to be right for the role. He or she needs you, or you wouldn't be seen in the first place.

If you are auditioning with another actor in a scene, don't let your partner's abilities or lack of abilities affect you in any way. Really good actors tend to raise the level for all actors, so it is a pleasure to audition with a really good actor. Keep in mind you are being auditioned on your merits. Be pleasant, keep that smile, don't be intimidated, and stay positive. You will need to relate to your partner, but don't worry about him or her. Keep your concentration on the task at hand.

An actor may be asked to perform a cold reading. In that instance, the actor will be presented a scene upon arrival, given only a few minutes to prepare (by returning to the waiting room or stepping outside in the hall), and then asked to perform. If an actor is auditioning at a cold reading, since the actor won't have much time to learn the lines, the casting director won't expect the actor to memorize the lines. Try to remember the first and last lines (the attention-getter and the closing) without looking at the script or copy. Casting directors need to know if an actor can think quickly and perform on his or her feet because it is not unusual to be given new materials at a casting session or, perhaps, on the set after you have booked the job. If your agent is able to get you the sides ahead of the audition, then you should try to learn as much of it as possible. It shouldn't seem as if this is the first time the actor has seen the sides. Be prepared! However, most casting directors will allow the actor to bring the sides into the audition room. Don't bury your face in the sides so that the camera and the casting director can't see your facial expressions.

Have fun at an audition. I love when one of my actors returns from an audition and says that he or she may not have been cast, but the audition was fun. When I was acting, if I knew that I did my best and had fun at the audition, that gave me satisfaction. Obviously, an actor wants to book the role, but there is nothing wrong with having fun at the audition. Treat every audition as a new learning experience.

Don't treat an audition as a "life or death" matter. That desperation will be noticed by the casting director/director/producer/client and could cost an actor the job. Relax! I especially like to tell the children and teens I represent to remember this: if you don't book the job, your parents, siblings, friends still will love you. No one will accuse you of being a horrible person because you didn't book that commercial or film. I once had an audition for my cousin Kim's daughter (my second cousin who was a child at the time). She went into the audition, and she came out of the room along with the casting director who went up to her mother (Kim) and asked if she could audition (the commercial was for a mother-daughter). Kim went into the audition completely relaxed and kept saying that she wasn't an actress. Guess what? Kim booked a regional commercial (unfortunately, her daughter didn't book it). I'm convinced Kim booked the commercial because she was so relaxed and natural.

As an agent, I will never knowingly send an actor on an audition where the actor has to do anything illegal or immoral, so the actor shouldn't be afraid to do what the casting director asks. For example, at one audition, a casting director asked an actor what her favorite food was. She replied that it was spaghetti, so the casting director told the actress to show him what spaghetti looked like. Without missing a beat, the actress waved her arms around to indicate wiggly spaghetti. There wasn't a right or wrong answer here; the casting director wanted to see how imaginative the actress was.

With that being said, an actor should not be subjected to anything that he or she considers degrading or immoral. The so-called "casting couch" from years ago is gone. No one should feel that he or she has to give sexual favors to get acting work. The #Me Too Movement was established as a way to encourage men and women to share their stories as part of an anti-sexual harassment movement. This movement broke the silence surrounding sexual harassment, sexual assault, and sexual bullying. If this happens to you at an audition or on a set, leave immediately, call the police, and call your agent. This should not happen to anyone in any line of work.

Regarding nudity in a film or for television, any nudity in a scene must be disclosed and agreed to before an actor accepts a role. An actor should not be pressured suddenly to disrobe while on an audition or on a set. If this should occur, calmly excuse yourself and call your agent or SAG-AFTRA representative immediately.

On a happier note, if an actor gets a callback, which means the director or client wants to see the actor a second time (this is good!), know the sides. For some auditions, such as commercials that may involve a lot of people, the director or the client may need to see the actor a second time. If 150 people auditioned in the first round, ten may be called back to audition a second time. This is usually a good sign, although not everyone who gets a callback will be chosen. It is also possible to be booked from the first audition. In the case of television and films, the director and producer(s) may want to see an actor a second or third time. For television, often the network has to give approval for an actor to be booked for a role. ALWAYS WEAR WHAT YOU WORE FOR THE FIRST AUDITION AT THE CALLBACK. The director liked something about the actor at the first audition and, perhaps, the wardrobe the actor wore attracted the director's attention, so wear the same clothes for the callback. I'm convinced I booked an industrial film years ago because of the blouse I wore. The blouse was a very simple, inexpensive blouse in a teal blue color. Every time I wore this blouse, I always received many compliments. I think it had to do with the bright teal color. Hopefully, my acting also was good.

Do not change your appearance from the way you looked for the first audition (don't cut your hair or shave your beard) until you find out if you have a callback. Then after the callback, don't change your appearance until you find out if you have booked the job. Also, unless your agent was given specific feedback from the casting director (this could happen), perform the role for the callback the same way you performed it at the first audition. If the director wants you to make adjustments, listen carefully so that you can make changes to your performance.

Don't call a casting director, director, or producer unless he or she has given a phone number to you, or has requested for you to call. Let your agent do her job!

Don't drop by an audition uninvited simply because you heard that someone was casting a movie, commercial, etc., or because a friend told you there was a role for which you should audition. THIS IS VERY UNPROFESSIONAL! However, certainly you could call your agent to tell him or her what your friend said. It is very possible that your agent submitted you for this project, but the casting director wasn't interested in having you audition for it. He or she may have felt that you just weren't right for this role.

One actor I represent complains constantly to me about not having auditions. She finally had two film auditions on back-to-back days; one was a video submission and one was an in-person audition. For the video audition, she couldn't get anyone to read the other role off-camera. For the live audition, she couldn't attend because she had car trouble; couldn't find a ride from anyone; and didn't have money for a taxi. Do these situations happen? Absolutely! What's the moral of this story? Life happens. Move on to the next audition, but do try to plan ahead for situations similar to what the above actor had. Also, don't complain to your agent about not getting auditions! I'll repeat that agents work very hard for their actors and want all actors to book as much work as possible.

SET ETIQUETTE

CONGRATULATIONS! YOU BOOKED THE JOB! ENJOY YOURSELF! WORKING IN A FILM, COMMERCIAL, VIDEO, TELEVISION SERIES, ETC., CAN BE LOTS OF FUN AS WELL AS A LEARNING EXPERIENCE!

Once you have booked acting work, your agent will tell you the good news. Then a person from the wardrobe department will contact you about when and where to go for a wardrobe fitting, for which you usually will be paid.

Your agent will tell you as much information about the job as he or she has, such as actual shooting days, location, etc. The Assistant Director will call you to introduce himself or herself. For a film or television show, you will be emailed the screenplay or script. For a commercial, if you have lines, you will be emailed the copy.

Depending on the size of the role that you have, you may be invited to a Table Read, which is exactly as it sounds. The actors who were cast introduce themselves, and then they sit around a table reading the screenplay or script.

This is very exciting, especially for beginning actors. The actor is able to hear the entire screenplay or script read aloud by the professional actors who were cast in the project.

It is also possible that an actor will be asked to rehearse with the director and the cast before the first day of filming. Depending on the size of an actor's role, the director may choose to rehearse on the set the first day the actor will film. For a television series, there is much more rehearsal time on the set (especially if the actor's role is large) before filming takes place.

When working in a film, video, commercial, etc., the actor should remember the following:

(1) Listen carefully to everything your agent tells you concerning wardrobe (the wardrobe person also will call you), location, directions, etc. The Assistant Director usually calls the actor, too, to tell you about locations. You will be emailed a production list and production schedule (usually referred to as "day of days" – DOD). This lists the different days that each scene or scenes will be shot. Later, as it gets closer to your filming day(s), you will be sent a call sheet with the time you need to report to the set. If you have any questions, ask your agent.

(2) When an actor books acting work, the actor usually doesn't find out the time and location of filming until the day before filming. Sometimes, the director is waiting to see how the weather will be (rain could affect filming). Also, the crew has to be given so much "down time." If a scene from the day before lasts longer than anticipated, that could affect the time of the next day's filming. Don't be alarmed! You will discover your call time eventually.

(3) Arrive on the set on time. THIS IS VERY IMPORTANT! Allow yourself enough time to get there. Keep in mind there is always traffic.

(4) Know your lines. Check every script you received (before the first filming day) to see if any changes were made.

(5)   Once you arrive, you usually will report to a production assistant (P.A.) to fill out paper work. Be sure to know your Social Security Number. Children under 18 usually will be asked to bring a birth certificate (or the birth certificate could have been requested before the actual filming day). Adults probably will be asked to bring at least one form of identification, such as a driver's license or passport, so have that with you. All talent on the set will be required to sign a release form, as well as tax forms. Talent under 18 must have the signature of a parent or guardian (this also could have been requested from a parent or guardian before the filming day). Children may need a work permit, too. You should know your agent's address and phone number; you may be requested to give this. I have had many actors call me while on the set because they need to supply my business address and phone number, and they can't remember what they are.

(6)   If you haven't already had a wardrobe fitting, you will be taken to wardrobe. If you did have a wardrobe fitting, your wardrobe will be in your trailer. Then you will be taken to hair and makeup. After hair and makeup, you will go to your trailer to relax and wait.

(7)   The actual contract will be waiting for the actor to sign in his or her trailer.

(8)   Listen carefully to everything you are told. The phrase "hurry up and wait" is used to describe a film, video, commercial, television set. An actor may have to arrive at 7:00 A.M. and might not be on set filming until 10:00 A.M. or later. Get used to this. It is the nature of the business.

(9)   If you leave your trailer for any reason (other than being called to the set), sit where you can easily be found when the director is ready for your scene. Do not leave the set until you are dismissed. If for some reason, it is necessary for you to leave before being officially dismissed, be sure to inform the P.A.

(10) You may want to bring something with you to occupy your time while you are waiting for your scene, such as a book to read. Children and teens may want to bring homework (or they may be tutored on the set; more information about that in another chapter).

(11) When you are first called to the set, this probably will be for a rehearsal. This is for logistical purposes so the director and DP (director of photography) can decide where everyone is standing, sitting, walking, etc., in the scene. The gaffer (in charge of lighting) may set up the lights at this time, and the sound technician may put a microphone on the actor. The actor may be told to return to the trailer, or may be asked to stay in the area if the crew is almost finished setting up.

(12) Do not complain about having to wait a long time. Directors do not like complainers. Also, don't complain about how small your trailer is or how uncomfortable your costume is. Be happy. Enjoy the opportunity you have been given to do what you love by being in a film, television show, etc. Not everyone gets this opportunity.

(13) Don't gossip or judge your fellow actors.

(14) Be polite and courteous to all people on the set. Just because you are an actor, this does not mean that you are any better than the people who are performing more menial tasks.

(15) Be sure that the P.A. knows that you are an actor with a speaking role (if that is the case). One of my actors was booked on a television show, and initially everyone thought he was an extra until he politely informed them he had a speaking role. (He received many apologies.)

(16) Bring a cell phone in case you need to make a phone call, but don't bring it on the set while you are filming (or keep it hidden and on "silent"). DON'T USE YOUR CELL PHONE OR A CAMERA TO TAKE PICTURES DURING FILMING.

(17) Do not post pictures of yourself, other actors, script pages, or pictures from the set on social media. This has become a huge issue lately, and the studios/networks are not happy about this.

(18) If you take special medications, bring them with you. Depending on how long the filming will take (often all day or night), you will be fed on the set (and the food is usually plentiful and good on most sets). However, if you are on a special diet and/or if you are constantly hungry, you may want to bring your own food or a snack. Lunch (even though it might not be the time you usually eat lunch) is served six hours after Crew Call, the time the crew has to report to the set. There are two types of food on the set: Catering (more elaborate meals, depending on the budget for the project) and Craft Services (basically, snacks). The P.A. will tell you where to go for food, but, if not, don't be afraid to ask for food. On a SAG-AFTRA production, the actor has to be fed.

(19) When on the set, listen to everything the director tells you. Often, the director may choose to shoot multiple takes. This doesn't mean the actor did anything wrong. Sometimes the director will want to film a scene from different angles, or will want to do many takes until he or she gets the perfect take. If there is something you don't understand, ask questions.

(20) If you or another actor should flub a line or hear a phone ring off-camera, don't react to that. Keep going until the director says, "Cut!" The best footage could be in that take. If you are acting in a play, keep going as if you didn't make a mistake (chances are the audience won't know you made a mistake unless you call attention to it).

(21) When you are dismissed from your first day of filming, you usually will be given your call time for the next day of filming, if you are working consecutive days. If you are working other days later on the shoot, the assistant director will get in touch with you with location and call time information, as it becomes available.

(22) Weeks or months later after filming has completed, an actor may be asked to record additional dialogue (ADR), for which the actor will go to a studio and record for about an hour or two. For actors with large roles, the ADR may last much longer, even multiple days or weeks. The actor will be paid for this. It doesn't mean the actor did anything wrong on the set during the original shoot. Perhaps, there was noise in the scene (an airplane over head; other outside noises), and the director wants to get more clarity.

(23) For a SAG-AFTRA project, the actor will be paid within a certain amount of days from the first shooting day. If you don't receive your pay check in a timely manner, contact your agent. For non-union projects, there is no written protocol for when the actor will be paid. However, for most non-union work, actors usually are paid within thirty days of the shooting of the project.

CHAPTER IV

So, What Do You Think Of My Face?
Real Acting Stories and Situations

One female actor had an audition for a feature film where she needed to portray a college student, riding on a streetcar with her boyfriend. In the scene an older man, who is intoxicated, gets on the streetcar, sits behind the couple, leans toward them, startles them, and asks the question, "So what do you think of my face?" Then the female actor responds with her line. The female actor I represented at the time attended the audition, met the casting director, was told to have a seat, and the casting director proceeded to chat with her. In the middle of chatting about the weather, the casting director asked the actor, "So what do you think of my face?," the cue line from the screenplay. The actor was startled (which could have worked for the scene), but she got totally thrown off and made it obvious she didn't realize the audition was starting then. I can't blame her for her reaction; however, I have since discovered that this particular casting director does this often. Actors, be ready for anything and everything at an audition. Go as prepared as you can be, but don't be surprised if something unusual happens, such as the above scenario. One of my actors in Florida auditioned for a television series, and the casting director, whom this actor didn't know, pretended to be the receptionist and engaged the actor in conversation. This could happen to you.

Another actor, Leon Contavesprie, was auditioning for the television series TREME for the role of record store manager. The director of the episode spoke with a thick foreign accent and started yelling at Leon (not in the script). Leon didn't flinch and said his line, "I told you to leave the record store." He was booked for the role. Some times directors want to catch an actor off guard to see how he or she will react.

Actor Michael Shane Hughes auditioned for a role on a television series. The casting director wasn't in a very good mood (that can happen) and actually yelled at Michael because he brought his headshot and resume (which weren't needed). Michael smiled, was courteous, had a positive attitude, auditioned as best as he could, and left. He called me that night and said he doubted that he would get cast. Guess what? Michael booked the role. I used this example with the high school students I was teaching at the time because some of the students were ready to fight anyone who looked at them the wrong way. I explained to them that regardless of how the interviewer (for a regular job) or the casting director (for acting work) may act toward them that they need to be pleasant and not make a face showing their displeasure. That's exactly how Michael conducted himself – not letting someone in a bad mood affect him – and he was hired for the role. It was a great teaching moment for me.

I told the first story in this chapter to actors at a workshop I taught, so these actors were prepared if a similar situation occurred at an audition. Actor Hilda Garrison was prepared to audition for a role portraying a pregnant woman. At her audition, the casting director, for whom she had auditioned for other productions, saw Hilda walking in the hall of the hotel (not in the audition room) and asked her when the baby was due (her cue line). Without a second thought, Hilda replied the baby was due in five months. She didn't get cast for this project, but at least she was prepared.

At some auditions, the casting director will hire a reader to read the other roles with the actor. Often this reader will be an actor (best case scenario), but, occasionally, the casting director will have the reader say the lines like a robot in a monotone with no expression at all. This can be difficult for an actor, but prepare for this possibility as well.

In another situation, actors were sent individual sides to prepare for an audition for a television series. When the actors arrived at the audition, the casting director decided that all actors would audition with the same sides. My actor and a few other actors were given new sides to prepare as they walked into the audition. The actors were allowed to walk outside the audition room to prepare. This is where training is important. My actor and the other actors had to make immediate choices, and my actor, who had taken many improvisation classes, felt comfortable in this situation.

Another actor I represent was driving to New Orleans from a city an hour away for a callback for a role in a "Movie of the Week." Before he arrived at the audition, the casting director called to tell me that the role had been eliminated from the script. The actor was very upset when he was told this; however, the casting director allowed him to audition for another role. The actor attempted to make the best of this disappointing situation.

I once taught a summer acting class for teenagers. I asked a casting director that I knew to attend one of the sessions and give some pointers to the attendees. He decided to conduct an audition as close to a real audition as possible. He videotaped the students and asked them questions. He asked one of the girls if she could sing. She said she couldn't. He replied that everyone can sing and that she should sing a simple song, like "Happy Birthday." The student refused. The casting director told her that she probably was a nice person, but he would never cast her in anything that he directed. She was somewhat appalled. His answer was he didn't ask if she could sing well, just if she could sing. He emphasized that actors need to follow directions and be prepared for anything at an audition.

Once again, actors, check your email daily. I recently had a non-union audition for a commercial shooting in New Orleans. I submitted actors who fit the roles. The casting director asked for nineteen of my actors to submit a video audition the next day. I promptly emailed each of the nineteen actors with all of the information. After a few hours, when some of the actors didn't respond to the email, I texted, and in some cases, telephoned the actors. Two actors who responded would be out-of-town for the shooting dates, so they weren't available, as well as two other actors who declined for health reasons. Seven actors submitted video auditions. Eight actors have yet to respond to the email, text, or phone call. There could be valid reasons, but this is very frustrating for agents. I'm not a magician!

Whether or not an actor gets booked for a role often is beyond the control of the actor. I have had actors lose roles because the producer's nephew was booked for the role. This happens. These two unusual situations occurred. One of my actors, Shane LeCocq, also owns a dance studio in Louisiana. He is a professional dancer/dance instructor in addition to being an actor. He auditioned for a role in a commercial, where the breakdown specified the actor had to be a dancer with a lot of dance experience. Shane fit the role perfectly. He got a callback, and the casting director had Shane dance with each woman who also got a callback. I was certain Shane would book this commercial, but, unfortunately, he didn't. At another audition a few weeks later, Shane saw the actor who booked the dance commercial and chatted with him. He asked the actor what dance experience he had, and the actor responded that he had never danced in his life. Strange! The second strange happening concerns my actor Rene J.F. Piazza, who booked a lot of non-union commercials before he became eligible for SAG-AFTRA. Rene had booked a series of commercials for this one local production company, and I knew this company liked using Rene for its commercials. When one of the commercial directors called me explaining that he needed an actor for an upcoming commercial, his words were, "I need a Rene Piazza type." I asked him if I could send Rene Piazza to audition for him, and he replied that would be great. You guessed it! Rene wasn't booked for the commercial.

Some times there is no rhyme or reason to how actors are booked for roles. Actors need to be eternal optimists that eventually if they audition enough, they will get booked for work.

Parents: Stage Moms and Advice to Parents

I have heard this from parents more times than I can count: "I know you hear this all the time, but my child really is beautiful." Please! Yes, your child should be beautiful to you, but that doesn't mean I think he or she is beautiful. Let me explain. All humans are beautiful within. However, it's my job as an agent to look for actors (children, teens, adults) who are talented and marketable. Your "beautiful" child may be cute and sweet and sing beautifully in your home, but he or she may clam up in front of a casting director and be uncooperative. Time is money. Directors and producers don't have time to waste, so if a child won't cooperate with a casting director, the casting director won't recommend the child to the director. The director doesn't want to have to replace an uncooperative child on a set.

Years ago before I was an agent, I actually auditioned with a child who mumbled during slating. He was a beautiful child whom I observed before the audition chatting in the hall and smiling at everyone. During slating, the casting director asked him three times to speak up, and his response was inaudible each time. On the fourth time, he screamed his name and had a sour-puss look on his face. What do you think his chances were of booking the commercial? Nada!

I pleasantly discovered that first impressions aren't always correct. I interviewed two adorable girls, ages four and nine, who were accompanied with their mother. The nine year old was well-behaved, but the four year old was running all around the room and not listening at all to her mom's response to behave. I thought to myself that there was no way I could send her on an audition; I doubted that she would listen to the casting director's directions, much less to the director on a set. However, both girls attended a workshop I taught. The nine year old behaved as expected. To my surprise, the four year old was well-behaved, very poised, and took direction from me very well. I am happy to say that she booked both a commercial and a film, and I received nothing but compliments about both her acting and behavior. The moral is first impressions can be wrong.

I once represented an adorable boy, age five, who was cast in a music video. The child was cooperative and took direction well. The problem was his mother. The mother fancied herself a singer and brought a CD she had recorded in her house to give to the singer in the video. That was bad enough, but she pestered the singer with numerous questions. When the mom was asked to refrain from conversing with the artist in the video, she caused a scene on set. The mom obtained the producer's phone number and called her at 3:00 A.M. to apologize for her behavior. She claimed her rude behavior was because she was going through a divorce. I was totally unaware of this until the producer, who was extremely nice, called me later to tell me that she loved the child in the video but the mother was outrageous. I'm lucky the producer didn't hold me responsible for the mother's behavior. End result: I'm no longer representing the little boy. Parents, don't try to promote your own career when accompanying your child on a set.

Another big problem regarding parents: Agents do their best to get auditions for all of their actors. Don't call your child's agent to complain that so and so (another child actor) had an audition and your child didn't. It's quite possible that your child was submitted for the movie or commercial or television show, but the casting director didn't think your child fit the role. This happens so often. Perhaps, your child has black hair, and the role was for a child with red hair.

Parents, mainly moms, are too ready to drop an agent if they think their child isn't getting enough auditions. I think I can speak for all agents in saying we work very, very hard for our actors. Parents should keep two things in mind: (1) Speaking for myself, I am an agent; I am not a production company. I have no control over whether or not a movie, commercial, etc., is filming in Louisiana (or anywhere else); and (2) Just because a movie, commercial, etc., is filming here, this doesn't mean that there is a role for your child (or for any child). Not all movies and commercials have children in them. Also, just because it's a Disney movie that doesn't mean there are automatically roles for children.

Parents, don't push your children. If it no longer is fun for children (or adults, too), they shouldn't audition. I was asked to give a presentation to parents at an acting school. The teacher had prepared each student thoroughly to audition for me with a scene that the teacher had worked on with each child. All children were ready to perform for me. One really cute little boy, age four, took one look at me and started crying. His mother and the acting teacher both said he had nothing to worry about, that he should perform the monologue the way he had practiced. He held tightly to his mother's leg and continued crying. His mother was very upset. I told her that her son was adorable, and I could tell that he was well-prepared, but I couldn't sign him because I couldn't risk having him cry and not be able to perform at an audition. I told the parent to wait until he was older, and he could perform for me then. Five years later I was at the same acting school, and the boy (whom I didn't recognize) was there and ready to perform for me. His performance was terrific. I signed him, and he already has performed in a commercial. Let children become actors when they are ready.

Ninety-nine per cent of the parents I deal with are wonderful. One special family, the Kristen and Shane Brooks family, whose five children I represent, are the most cooperative people with whom I have ever worked. If I called Kristen and told her I had an audition for one of her children, and they had to arrive at the audition in two hours, Kristen would find a way to make it work. I might also add that she is a teacher, so it's not that easy to drop everything to take one of the children to an audition, but she would do that. I realize not all parents are able to drop everything to take their children to an audition, and, fortunately, most casting directors will give actors more time to get to an audition, but in this business, a parent may need to get a child quickly to an audition. Hats off to those parents who cooperate. You make my job easier.

Parents, do not bring sick children to an audition. I know you are excited when your child has an audition, but don't risk infecting other children (and adults) by bringing your sick child to an audition. Plus, your child will be cranky and not at his or her best. If at all possible, please don't bring a sibling or another child (other than the child who is auditioning) with you to an audition. Often the waiting rooms are small, and there is not a lot of room for extra people. Absolutely, don't bring another sick child with you.

Parents, also tell your agent before the audition if your child has an injury. One child I represent had broken her arm a few days before the audition. The parent wisely informed me. I informed the casting director who said the child should not attend this audition. One of my actors booked a commercial where the child who was supposed to be in the scene with him (not from my agency) had broken her leg. The parent didn't inform her agent and brought the child to the set. Needless to say, the commercial had to be reworked, and no one on the set was happy about this.

If you agree to take your child on an audition and something happens (illness, accident, car trouble, etc.), call your agent as soon as possible. I called a parent whose child was scheduled for an early morning audition for a film to inquire about how the audition went. The mom told me her daughter didn't go because she was ill. I found this out long after the child's scheduled audition time. The parent should have called me to inform me of this. Good communication is very important.

I said this earlier in the book, but because it's so important, I will repeat: Parents, let your agent know if your child has any kind of allergy, for example, an allergy to nuts, as some children (and adults) have. I was prepared to send one of my child actors for an audition for one of the college football conferences. In the commercial, the child had to eat a certain candy bar. The casting director was not aware that the candy bar had nuts in it.

Fortunately, my actor's grandmother researched the product and discovered it has nuts, particularly tree nuts, in it. Her grandson is highly allergic to tree nuts. I relayed this information to the casting director, so other child actors wouldn't attend the audition if they had allergies to tree nuts.

Parents, get these items together in anticipation of your child's getting cast in a movie, television show, commercial, etc.:

(1) Social Security Card (a copy is acceptable; not the original);

(2) Birth Certificate (a copy);

(3) Possibly a work permit;

(4) Sometimes a copy of the most recent report card:

(5) Production will send a Parental Consent Form to the agent, and the agent will send that to the parent.

RULES FOR MINORS ON A SET:

According to professional set tutor Sue-Dee Lazzerini, a legal guardian (either a parent or an adult with a notarized document stating legal guardianship) is required to be with the minor AT ALL TIMES. This is to protect the child and the production. This is what is required by law.

A child must be accompanied to wardrobe and when wired for sound by a parent, guardian, or the studio teacher (also known as set tutor).

A child shouldn't go anywhere alone. Clothes (wardrobe) will be put in a room (usually a trailer) on a hanger.

Parent, guardian, or set tutor must accompany the child to make-up.

If a child works on set two or more days in a thirty-day period, the child must be tutored for three hours each day that he or she works on the set. Failure to do this can result in a huge fine for the production company. However, if a child under the age of 18 works only one day, he or she doesn't need to be tutored.

Please note:

The adults who are studio teachers (set tutors) are experienced certified teachers with a lot of teaching experience. The tutors often give tests to actors, if asked to do this.

The set tutors first ask if the child actors have assigned work from their schools and will work on that first. However, if a child doesn't bring any work and the regular school teacher doesn't send any work, the set tutor usually has work to give the child.

I always tell young actors how important it is to keep up with their studies so the teachers and principals at their regular schools won't complain that the actors have to miss school for acting work. Most are delighted that their students are involved in a film, television show, or commercial.

For child actors in Louisiana, set tutors must teach according to the school schedule of the parish where the movie, television show, etc., is being shot. If the project is being shot during vacation time in that particular parish, the child actor does not need to be tutored at that time.

If a child actor in a movie, television show, etc., is from New York or California, their schools usually are still in session during the early part of the summer (whereas, Louisiana students start the school year earlier and end the school year earlier). The child actors from New York or California still would be tutored.

Legally, set tutors in Louisiana don't have to tutor during the summer. However, most directors ask set tutors to work "welfare" in the summer. The set tutor would follow the child actors on the set and remain with them. There is no welfare requirement in Louisiana, but there are welfare requirements in New York and California.

Also, for children under eighteen who work on a film or television show, other than as an extra, the parent must set up a Coogan Trust Account, where the producer (employer) is required to deposit 15% of gross earnings directly into the minor's Coogan Trust Account. Only certain banks can be used to set up these accounts, so parents should consult their agents about this.

Background information about the Coogan Act:

Child actor Jackie Coogan (1914-1984) once held the record of being the youngest millionaire in history, earning an estimated four million dollars as a child actor. Unfortunately, in those days there were no restrictions as to how children in film were to be treated. In 1938, Jackie learned that his mother and step-father had spent most of his fortune. Jackie had to sue them for what was left of his earnings. The court decided that Jackie had no right to his income due to his age at the time he earned it. Public uproar caused California to pass "The Coogan Act" in 1938, which was revived in 2004. Because of this law, a minor's earnings are the separate property of the child, and producers have to deposit 15% of a child actor's gross earnings into a Coogan Trust Account. The child actor is able to receive the money from the account when he or she reaches adulthood or becomes legally emancipated.

Working on a film, television series, commercial, etc. can be very beneficial for children. In addition to being fun, hopefully, for a child, children learn cooperation, commitment, discipline, and a sense of accomplishment. As an agent, I am happy to represent child actors.

CHAPTER VI

Film, Television, and Theatre Glossary; Important Terms That Actors Should Know

(1) Acting Bug – The slang term used to indicate that someone of any age has been infected with a great desire to be an actor.

(2) Action – The cue that is shouted by the director when the camera starts rolling.

(3) Actor – A person who performs on stage, in films, or on television.

(4) Actors' Equity Association – AEA – also known as Equity; the union for professional theatre actors.

(5) Actor's Reel – A compilation of clips from an actor's career; can aid an actor in booking more jobs.

(6) A.D. – Assistant Director

(7) ADR – Additional Dialogue Recorded; also known as Automated Dialogue Replacement; also known as Looping – When an actor's dialogue is not recorded correctly, it needs to be re-recorded.

(8) Agent – Person responsible for the professional business dealings of an actor. Agents typically negotiate contracts on behalf of

the actors. Agents submit headshots and resumes to the Casting Director.

(9) Arena Stage – In a theatre, a performance space in which the audience sits all around the stage; sometimes called "Theatre In-The-Round."

(10) Art Director – Second in charge of the Art Department after the Production Designer. The Art Director "mirrors" the look of the film, which includes sets, costumes, make-up, props, locations, and construction.

(11) Articulation – The clear and precise pronunciation of words.

(12) Audition – An interview-like opportunity in which actors are able to demonstrate their talents, meet the person hiring the cast, and leave impressions of themselves.

(13) Avail – A courtesy situation extended by an agent to a producer, indicating that a performer is available to work a certain job. Avails have no legal or contractual status.

(14) Background Actors – Also referred to as "Extras"; actors with no lines.

(15) Backstage – The entire area behind the stage of a theatre, including dressing rooms.

(16) Base Camp – The area where the trailers for the actors are located, usually close to the set; this also refers to the area where "extras" wait before being called to the set.

(17) Best Boy – Also known as Assistant Chief Lighting Technician; the head electrician responsible for getting power to the set. The Best Boy works for the Gaffer.

(18) Billing – The order of the names in the titles or opening credits of a film or television show or on a theatre marquee.

(19) Bio (or Biography) – A resume in narrative form, usually for a printed program or press release.

(20) Blocking – The director's planned movements for actors on stage, in film, and in television, including entrances, exits, and any steps taken in any direction.

(21) Body Language – Bodily movements, large or small, which indicate what a person is thinking or feeling.

(22) Booking – A firm commitment to a performer to do a specific job. If you are "booked," you got the role!

(23) Boom – An overhead microphone, often used on set, usually mounted on an extended pole that points toward the actors.

(24) Boom Operator – Person who handles the boom microphone for the Sound Recordist or Mixer.

(25) Breakdown – A detailed listing and description of roles available for casting in a production; a description of each character and the character's place in the plot.

(26) Broadway – New York City's principal theatre district; the theatre capital of the world.

(27) Buyout – An offer of full payment in lieu of residuals, when the contract permits; often used for non-union commercial work.

(28) Callback – An invitation for an actor to return for a second audition. ALWAYS WEAR THE SAME CLOTHES YOU WORE FOR THE FIRST AUDITION. Usually, the director (for a film or television show) or the client (for a commercial) is present at the callback.

(29) Call Sheet – Production term for the daily listing of the shooting schedule, scenes, and the cast involved.

(30) Call Time or Call – The time the actor is due on set. For stage actors, this is the time the actor must report to the theatre for a performance.

(31) Casting Director – The person responsible for supplying actors for the film, television show, or play. The Casting Director contacts

the agents with the breakdowns, looks over agent submissions, and then requests actors to audition.

(32) Caterer – Person or company that provides the main meals for cast and crew, either on set or on location.

(33) Cattle Call – A large open audition; often known as an "open call." Actors don't need to have an agent to attend a cattle call; however, if you do have an agent, you should list the agent's name on any paper work you fill out.

(34) Character Role – A supporting role with pronounced or eccentric characteristics.

(35) Chemistry – A mysterious element that creates excitement when two actors appear together.

(36) Choreographer – An artist who designs (choreographs) dances for the stage or screen.

(37) Cinematographer – The person who designs the way each shot in a film should be lit and filmed.

(38) Climax – The turning point of the story; the last time the protagonist and antagonist clash.

(39) Close-Up (CU) – Camera term for a tight shot of the shoulders and face.

(40) Cold Reading – An unrehearsed reading of a scene, usually at auditions. Some casting directors choose not to release the "sides" or "copy" until the actor arrives at the audition.

(41) Color-Blind Casting – Casting without regard to the race or ethnicity of the characters or actors.

(42) Commedia Dell 'Arte – A professional form of theatre developed in Italy in the 1500s; known for Stock Characters and Improvisation.

(43) Commissions – Money paid to agents for their services.

(44) Community Theatre – a local theatre group in a city or town.

(45) Composite – A one-sheet of photos representing an actor's different "looks."

(46) Conflict – Status of being paid for services in a commercial for one advertiser; thereby, contractually preventing an actor from performing in a commercial for a competitor. As an acting term, conflict is the confrontation of the protagonist against the antagonist.

(47) Continuity – In film or television, the coherence from shot to shot in the same scene.

(48) Copy – The script for a commercial or voice-over.

(49) Costume – Any clothing an actor wears for a performance.

(50) Costume Designer – The person who designs costumes to build or chooses costumes to rent, borrow, or buy for a production.

(51) Cover; Coverage – Shooting a scene from several directions.

(52) Craft Service – One of the most important jobs on the film for maintaining crew morale; this person has the snacks, sodas, coffee, etc., available close to the set.

(53) Cue – A line of dialogue, action, or sound, onstage or off, that tells an actor it is time to enter, exit, move across stage, or – most commonly – begin speaking.

(54) Curtain Up – The start of a theatre performance, whether or not an actual curtain exists in front of the stage.

(55) Dallies – Screening of footage in a film before it is edited.

(56) Day-player – A performer hired for a film or television series on a day-to-day basis, rather than under a long-term contract.

(57) Denouement – The final resolution of the conflict in a plot. (I love to pronounce this word.)

(58) Diaphragm – The lower part of the lungs, filling the abdominal space, that supports the voice when actors and singers breathe

correctly on stage. Diaphragmatic breathing is a great way to relax before performing.

(59) Diction – Clear, sharp pronunciation of words, especially of consonants.

(60) Director – In theatre, the person who oversees the entire process of staging a production; the director works with the actors to get the actors to interpret their lines accurately. In film, the director must work with the actors and technicians so that her/his vision for the scene is conveyed properly to the audience. The director is responsible for the film's artistic and creative aspects.

(61) Double-take – An exaggerated facial response to another actor's words or actions, usually used for comic effect.

(62) Downgrade – Reduction of a performer's on-camera role from principal to extra.

(63) Downstage – In a theatre, the area of the stage that is closest to the audience. It is important for an actor to know this when the director blocks a scene.

(64) D.P. – Director of Photography; also known as Cinematographer; responsible for the film's look.

(65) Dress Rehearsal – The final phase of rehearsals for a play before an opening night performance; actors are in full costumes.

(66) Dress the Set – To add items or props to the set.

(67) Emancipated Minor – A minor under 18 who has been given the status of a legal adult by a judge.

(68) Employer of Record (EOR) – The company responsible for employment taxes and unemployment benefits.

(69) Episode 102 – First season; Second episode. This is an example of what is listed for television episodes.

(70) Executive Producer – Person responsible for funding a production.

(71) EXT. (Exterior) – A scene shot outside.

(72) Farce – A comedy with exaggerated characterization, abundant physical or visual humor, and often an improbable plot.

(73) Flop – A theatrical production that fails to draw an audience, regardless of whether the critics liked it or not.

(74) Foundation – Makeup applied to the entire face to provide a base of uniform color.

(75) Gaffer – Works with D.P. and is responsible for lighting the scene. The Gaffer knows lighting and lighting equipment inside and out.

(76) Gesture – An expressive movement of the body or limbs.

(77) Going Up On A Line – Forgetting your next line.

(78) Greasepaint – The term used for all theatrical makeup, which was originally grease-based.

(79) Grip – The backbone of the production, the Grip works with the lighting department and the camera team. She/He is responsible for the camera supports, rigging, moving equipment, and assisting in the production.

(80) Ham – An actor who gives a very broad or exaggerated performance.

(81) Hiatus – Time when a TV series is in between production.

(82) Hold – A contractual obligation for a performer to be available for work.

(83) Holding Fee – Set payment by an advertiser to retain the right to use a performer's services, images, or likeness on an exclusive basis.

(84) Honeywagon – The trailer for most day players; this trailer usually is divided into five private dressing rooms and is very small. Enjoy it!

(85) Improvisation – Acting without rehearsing; on-the-spot.

(86) Industrial – Non-broadcast film; often educational films.

(87) INT. (Interior) – A scene shot indoors.

(88) In the Can – This term comes from the days when film was put in cans after it was shot; it means that the shot is completed to everyone's satisfaction.

(89) In Time – The actual call time or start time; also refers to return time from a break.

(90) Larynx – The human voice box, containing the vocal chords.

(91) Master Shot – A shot that includes everyone in the scene.

(92) Meal Penalty – A set fee paid by the producer for failure to provide meals on set as set by the contract.

(93) Method Acting (also known as Stanislavski Method) – An introspective method of acting developed by Russian director Constantin (also spelled Konstantin) Stanislavski (1863-1938) that requires actors to look inside themselves to find the motivation they need to portray a character accurately. Three questions an actor should ask in preparing for a scene: (1) What do I want?; (2) What stands in my way from getting what I want?; (3) How do I go about getting what I want?

(94) Moment Before – The moment before the scene begins; it helps if the actor can figure out what is happening before the scene begins.

(95) Monologue – A solo scene used by an actor to demonstrate his or her ability at an audition.

(96) Nice Casual – A wardrobe description given for an audition, which means to look presentable in a non-distracting way.

(97) Objective – What an actor's character wants in a scene.

(98) Off-Book – When an actor knows his or her lines and no longer needs to carry the script.

(99) Out Time – The actual time after which an actor has changed out of wardrobe and is released.

(100) Overtime – Work extending beyond the contractual workday.

(101) P.A. – Production Assistant – The runners or gophers on the set. The P.A.'s job may consist of holding back onlookers, getting coffee, and/or escorting actors to the location on a film or television set.

(102) Pan – A camera shot which sweeps from side to side. This term also can refer to a very bad review of a play or movie from a critic.

(103) Pantomime – To act without words through facial expression and gesture.

(104) Pausing for Effect – A deliberate pause within or between lines, used by an actor to call special attention to a moment.

(105) Period Piece – A project set in another era.

(106) Pick-Up – An added take because of a problem with a shot.

(107) Pilot – The first show of a possible television series, introducing the characters and situations for a potential series.

(108) Plot – All the action in a play, including the exposition, climax, and denouement. In a film or television series, this usually is referred to as the "storyline."

(109) Plus One – A guest to an invitation-only event or party.

(110) POV Shot – A point-of-view shot; camera angle from the perspective of one actor.

(111) Presence – An actor's ability to command attention onstage, even when surrounded by other actors.

(112) Principal – A performer with lines or special business, which advances the storyline; in a commercial, an actor who is a principal doesn't always have lines but is very visible on-camera.

(113) Producer – The person responsible for the day-to-day decisions on a production; responsible for raising funding, hiring key personnel, and arranging for distributors.

(114) Projection – An actor's ability to use his or her voice so that it can

be heard clearly in the back rows of a theatre; also used in reference to the emotions an actor wishes to convey.

(115) Props – Any movable object, from a letter to a sword, used by an actor during a performance.

(116) PROSCENIUM STAGE – A performance space in which the audience views the action on stage as if through a picture frame.

(117) Range – The vocal extent of a singer's voice, from its lowest note to it highest.

(118) Rave – An extremely good review from a critic.

(119) Read-Through – A complete reading of a play aloud by the assembled cast, usually at the first rehearsal.

(120) Residuals – Money owed to an actor each time a film, television show, or commercial runs on TV or is sold as a DVD.

(121) Re-write – Changes in the script for a film or television show; often made using color-coded pages.

(122) Role – A part in a play, film, or television show.

(123) Scale – Minimum payment for actors under Union contracts.

(124) Scale + 10 – Minimum payment for actors, plus 10% to cover agent's commission.

(125) SAG-AFTRA – Screen Actors' Guild-The American Federation of Television and Radio Artists – Now one union for professional film, television, and commercial actors.

(126) Screenplay – The text of a film.

(127) Script – The text of a play.

(128) Script Supervisor – Crew member who keeps track of how many takes are made of each shot and scene; how long they ran; who was in them; what lines of dialogue are changed, etc.

(129) Sense Memory – Memories of sights, sounds, smells, tastes, and textures, used to help define a character in a certain situation. Note:

You may have to portray a scene on stage or film unlike anything you have experienced, but everyone experiences various emotions. Tap into the emotion (even though the scene is different) when preparing for a role. Also, you may have to eat something on stage that isn't what it seems. Example: If you have to eat a "delicious chicken dinner" on stage and you don't like chicken, focus on a food you do like, and pretend that is what you are eating on stage. Use your "senses" to do this.

(130) Sides – A piece of the script or screenplay used for an audition for television or a film.

(131) Sight-and-Sound – Parents' rights, under Union contracts, to be within the sight of the child performer at all times.

(132) Signatory – An employer who has agreed to produce under the terms of a Union contract.

(133) Slating – At a taped audition, the actor gives his/her name, agent, and any other information the casting director requests, while standing on his/her "mark," a piece of tape on the floor.

(134) Spine – The essential motivation of the character.

(135) Stand-in – Person who looks like the main actor, especially in height, weight, and coloring, and stands on set for the lighting and camera set-ups (before the main actor arrives on set).

(136) Station 12 – At SAG-AFTRA, the office responsible for clearing SAG-AFTRA members to work.

(137) Storyboards – In a commercial, the story drawn out like a comic strip of the shots. For a film or television show, the different scenes in the order they will be shot are put on a poster-type board.

(138) Studio Teacher (also referred to as "Set Tutor") – The tutor hired to provide education to performers under 18; usually responsible for enforcing Child Labor Laws.

(139) Stunt Coordinator – Person responsible for designing and

supervising the performance of stunts and hazardous activities on a set. Stunt Performers work with the Stunt Coordinator.

(140) Subtext – Information that is implied but not stated by a character; thoughts or actions of a character that do not express the same meaning as the character's spoken words; the "hidden" meanings in the words of the character. Actors use tone of voice and body language to show subtext.

(141) Table Read – A read-through of a film by the cast, which sits around a table; actors are invited to attend this.

(142) Take – The clapboard indication of a shot "taken" or printed.

(143) Take 5 – The announcement of a periodic five-minute break.

(144) Thespian – A term for an actor; named after the Greek actor/playwright THESPIS, who is considered to be the first actor.

(145) Thrust Stage – A combination of the arena and proscenium stages, with the audience sitting on two or three sides of the acting area; often like a "beauty-pageant-type stage."

(146) Typecast – Playing the same role over and over.

(147) Upstage – The area of the stage in a theatre that is farthest from the audience; area near the backdrop.

(148) Wardrobe – The clothing a performer wears on camera.

(149) Working Actors – Actors who make a living acting.

(150) Work Permit – A legal document required to allow a child to work, issued by various state or local agencies.

(151) Wrap (or "That's a wrap!") – The production has finished filming.

(152) Zoom – Technique used on computers for video auditions, where the actor and casting director can communicate.

Sample Resume and Headshot

SCOTT SMITH

HEIGHT:	WEIGHT:	HAIR:	EYES:	AGENT:
6'2"	195 lbs.	Black	Green	HALE TALENT
				(504) 123-4567

AGE RANGE: 18-28

EDUCATION: Acting I - Tulane University
Acting for the Camera – taught by Dr. Rebecca Hale

ACTING EXPERIENCE:

Theatre
Death of a Salesman . . . . . . Biff . . . . BelAir High School, Houston, Texas
Of Mice and Men . . . . .Lenny. . . . . .Tulane University, New Orleans, LA

Film
Ray. . . . . Band Member . . . Co-star . . . . . .Directed by Taylor Hackford

Television
NCIS: NEW ORLEANS . . . . . Navy Sailor . . . . .Supporting....Directed by Lee Jones

Commercials
Popeye's Fried Chicken . . . .(Principal) . . . . (Regional)
Home Depot . . . . (Principal) . . . . (National)

Educational Video
"Fire Prevention . . . . Narrator . . . . Syndistar, Inc.

Music Video
Britney Spears . . . . .Man in Car

Print
Ford Motor Company . . . . . . .Man Driving Car . . .Company Brochure

Runway Modeling
Macy's Department Store

SPECIAL SKILLS:

Member of college varsity football team; licensed car driver; speaks French fluently; owns a tuxedo;

Waterskiing; karate; professional ballroom dancer; swimming; boxing; drummer in band

ABOUT THE AUTHOR

D r. Rebecca Hale has been a talent agent since 1994. Her agency, Hale Talent, represents actors all over the United States. Dr. Hale has a Ph.D. in Educational Theatre from New York University. She also has a Bachelor of Arts in English Education and a Master of Arts in Drama and Communications from the University of New Orleans. She taught theatre, English, and speech for forty-three years in high school, middle school, and college and has directed over seventy-five p lays. S he continues to teach acting classes and workshops. Dr. Hale resides in New Orleans, Louisiana.

Dr. Hale is the author of *The Soul of the City: Le Petit Théâtre du Vieux Carré of New Orleans.*

CPSIA information can be obtained
at www.ICGtesting.com
Printed in the USA
LVHW080612251121
704427LV00010B/950